A TODDLER MAMA'S JOURNEY IN PRAYER

HOLD ME, GOD SERIES BOOK 3

BRITNEY DEHNERT

Britney Dehnert
BOOKS

britneydehnertbooks@gmail.com

www.Britneydehnertbooks.com

Cover design by Patrick and Robin Wood.

A Toddler Mama's Journey in Prayer: Hold Me, God Series / Britney Dehnert. -- 2nd ed.

For Aravis,
who was a toddler not that long ago
and is now embarking on a new journey.
I love you, my precious daughter.

WHEN THEY'RE OLDER

*W*hen my girls are older
We won't have the diaper corner
taking up space.
　When they're older
　Toys won't litter the floor.
　When my babies are taller
　We can have an ordered, beautiful living room.
　When the fruit of my womb is grown
　My home can look like a magazine.

And?
　I'll long for the baby cuddles of today
　Chubby thighs that traverse the dirty floor
　in wide, bold steps
　Goldfish snacks and half-eaten apples,
　crunched by tiny, pearly teeth
　behind contented baby grins.
　Screams of laughter and gurgles of glee
　Restless lurches across the couch
　Tiny pattering feet that take them to places of
wonder

that together we glimpse through imagination
An age when it's easy to create games - in an instant
When "chase" and "hide" are the thrill of the day
When it's Mama and Daddy they cry for when they fall
When bedtime hugs and kisses are given with abandon and smacks of joy
And I can smooth soft baby curls
from their foreheads as they sleep.

This time of simple joy
    big feelings
    sparkling curiosity
    wild giggling
    is not to be traded for a picture-perfect house.
    Repellant thought!
    I give that idol to You now
    And I thank You
    for my precious, joyful girls
    and this unique and special time.
    Thank You for helping me treasure it.

SUBMISSION

*I*t's a choice:
         submission
A choice I often reject
First rejecting You
Then him.
I don't feel this loss,
this loss of connection
because of him
No.
I feel the loss
as a pang
a dull ache
a longing
because I keep the knife in my chest.

The knife is my refusal.
    The knife is my rejection.
    The knife is pride:
    I know better than he does.
    I do things better than he does.
    I notice more than he does.

The knife is resentment:
I've taken on more than he has.
I've blindly plunged it in
inch by inch
noticing symptoms now and then
shoving it further in while pointing my finger
at him.

Oh Creator,
I want to lead
Because I'm more efficient!
More of a leader!
All these things the knife whispers
as it digs.
But You made every bit of me
And every bit of him
And You planned the dance
And You made us partners.
So here, after ten years,
as I sit with a knife in my chest
I beg You to dig it out
fling it away!
where I cannot find it again.

The steps of the dance
that I first falteringly learned
twelve years ago
bring back to my muscle memory:
I want to trust *You* enough
that I can then trust *him*.

Cure the wound in my center,

clean it out with gentle love,
bind it closed with pure humility,
heal it over with grateful respect.

You are the Healer
    The Maker of New
    The Forger of Connection
    The Source of Love and Humility.
    Guide my steps, Kindest Master
    May I look to You,
    Great Lord of our dance.

YOU DON'T HAVE TO

*M*y Father, my God,
      I've felt winded lately
in my soul, in my heart.
What is it, God?
This feeling of stress
That's choked my throat
Filled my eyes?

You reveal now to me:
    "You don't have to get it right.
    I'm here for that."
    Thank You.
    That's the heart of it, isn't it?
    Your'e here
    You're purifying me
    I don't have to do everything
    efficiently to perfection
    I don't have to "get it all right."
    If I look to You
    Rest in You
    Ask You

Get strength, patience, wisdom
from You
All is well.
I shouldn't try to muster it all on my own -
For *You* are here.
And You've gotten it right for me already.

AWE

*O*h God, Your majesty!
    How quickly I forget
Though I see it out my window
In every corner, every step.
I can't find the rhymes to praise You
But I giggle because You don't mind
If my words are stellar or inspiring -
No, that doesn't matter now
Because after all, the point is You!
So as my thoughts run and scatter
You go on and on
Glorious beyond all thoughts!

You taught the bees to dance
    The flowers to open for the sun and go to bed
at night.
    You programmed the squirrel to plan
    For a season far away
    And speaking of far:
    How many animals did You create
    To migrate every year?

Some cross oceans, others continents
Many go further than people travel in a year
And they go without faltering
Because of knowledge that *You* put in them.

The stars, planets, celestial bodies
Turn to a unique, rhythmic *sound*!
We can hear it with invented instruments
Because You put in us
The desire to find out, to discover
And You added the abilities to do so!
All of us so different!
And when we put our gifts together,
Planets can be reached
Ocean depths discovered
Microbes seen
Colors created
Music composed
Heart-reaching words painted
Wonders built.
You made it all -
From the hormones to the tiny germs
From the planetoids to the comets
To inspiration and mathematical genius
To rhythm and invention.
You are indescribably beyond my mind.

Thank You for Your grace to me,
Your wayward daughter.
Thank You, Creator.

A PSALM 131 CRY

O Lord, my heart is not lifted up;
*   my eyes are not raised too high;*
I do not occupy myself with things
*   too great and too marvelous for me.*
But I have calmed and quieted my soul,
*   like a weaned child with its mother;*
*   like a weaned child is my soul within me.*
O Israel, hope in the Lord
*   from this time forth and forevermore.*
(Psalm 131 ESV)

My LORD, my Creator and Father and Savior,
    My heart *is* proud
    and I'm in the thick of things too difficult
for me
    that I've created myself:
    deadlines and projects
    expectations and stresses
    too difficult for my mind and body
    and I'm trying to force my way through
anyway.

. . .

But You offer me rest!
    You offer me real peace
    You offer Your embrace
    like a nurturing, gentle mother
    for me to crawl to
    no matter how frantic
    or sheepish
    I feel.
    You're here
    guiding my steps
    even when I've lost my time
    and I can't keep up with my own expectations
    and I feel like running
    running
    running
    like a wild woman
    until it's *all done.*

But running myself into the ground
    won't bring me peace,
    won't help my sweet family.
    No.

But instead,
    resting in You
    remembering You've got this
    You're ordering my circumstances
    You're making my mess the best for me.

It's not the results of my striving that You're after.

It's what turns me to You that changes me
- and circumstances -
for good.

A SERVANT HEART

"*G*reater love has no one than this, that one should lay down his life for his friends" (John 15:13 BLB).

I've always thought of laying down my life
as death - for another - the ultimate sacrifice.

But I realize now

As You teach me about having a servant heart

That though I would willingly die to save my daughters, my husband, my family, and my friends…

You call me daily to lay down my life in a different way.

Lay down my idols of comfort and cultural "success"

Lay down my wishes for myself

Lay down my emotions that betray me-centered beliefs.

You don't call me to do *great things* in this life;

You call me to do *the* great things in this life:

"…love the Lord your God with all your heart

and with all your soul and with all your mind...
And...You shall love your neighbor as yourself"
(Matthew 4:37-39 ESV).

To love my family as myself
Will You help me every minute, every hour?
To lay down my life
To focus on their needs
Especially their need for You
- their need to know You and Your Word -
And know that You will fill me up
give me all I need
As I draw from You
to give them all I have
keeping none in reserve for myself
but instead taking the time to draw from You
because You give me all I need.

THE KEY TO MY CHAINS

*S*elf-sacrifice, a servant heart:
　　The keys to my chains!
You show me the freedom
Of leaving self-first behind!
If I start with me,
That brings frantic scrambling and clinging
Even while caring for others,
"I gotta help myself!"
It shrieks at the side
While I change diapers and read
Fetch milk and toys.
With a me-gremlin screaming
It's harder to love
Harder to serve
Easier to stress
And complain
And feel sorry for me.

But You've handed me the keys
　　You've shown me the chain
　　I'm ready to loose the lock

And let the change begin.

A servant heart, LORD,
    Is what I desire now
    Remake this gremlin one, I pray
    Make me like Jesus,
    Washing filthy feet
    Speaking gently,
    Giving grace,
    Living humbly.
    I want to be like You.
    Will You show me the freedom?
    Take away my fear?
    Let me find the true me
    That You created me to be
    A servant,
    Like Jesus.

THE FIGHT

Father God,
      I have felt so crushed
defeated
frustrated
at the marching of my sin.
Continual battle has worn me down
My weapon hangs heavy in my hands,
then droops by my side.
My head bows in anticipated defeat
as I think,
"Even if I push them off now
Even if today a break-through happens
Give it a month
Satan will be back
The enemy will sneak in behind me
Make his attack when I'm confident and happy
And then I'm losing again.

O God,
    Is it even worth it?
    This constant battle for my soul?

You saved me
Set me on a rock
You stand by my side
Sacrificed all
But he keeps coming back.

And God,
As even my emotions
My hormones
That You made
That should fight on *my* side,
Join his camp
And turn on me:
Traitors in my own body.
I'm tired, Captain.
I'm worn.
I'm sick of this battle.

I have so much good in my life
You've blessed me beyond sight
Yet still I fall under discontent
And sink, writhing, in the fight.
Why can't I just see the good?
And thank You every day?
Why can't I tame my body down?
And calm my heart before it strays?
And here I'm prattling on and on
Not listening to Your voice...

"Be still and know that I AM God
And I will have the victory.
You are My child, my beloved one

Over you the angels sing.
The fight is worth your fight
But so much more is clear
The fight will point you here to Me
Where you can rest, lay down your heart.
Come to My arms, My precious one
Give to Me your despair
I'll heal your wounds, soothe your pain
Give you grace beyond compare."

OK, God, I'll nestle in
Trust that You'll provide
The weapons, the win, the rest I need
And that You'll never leave my side.

THE WINDS

"... *So that we may no longer be children, tossed to and fro by the waves and carried about by every wind of doctrine, by human cunning, by craftiness in deceitful schemes*" (Ephesians 4:14 ESV).

"*He said to them, 'Where is your faith?' And they were afraid, and they marveled, saying to one another, 'Who then is this, that he commands even winds and water, and they obey him?'*" (Luke 8:25 ESV).

Your kindness, God, is glorious!
    Your love for me is sure.
    I will sing here of Your faithfulness
    Of how Your patience will endure.
    My own goes up and down all day
    Receding with the very wind
    Yet with You the winds hold no sway
    And at Your word the gales rescind.
    The winds 'round here, are fast and strong
    But oh, You're much stronger still
    Even fire tornadoes have no sway

When a look from You will make them chill.
A lift of Your finger chills their heat
And will stop them in their tracks
But surprised I will not be
For I have seen Your mighty acts.
So even here in this crazy time
As bad winds blow on every side
Despite the hate and fear and fire
Your promises will still abide.

ALL I'VE GOT

"*For great is your love, reaching to the heavens; your faithfulness reaches to the skies*" (Psalm 57:10 NIV).

God,
    When I don't know what to pray
    Or how to calm my heart
    When I don't know what I need
    Or even where to start
    You lead me back to the Psalms
    To the Rock much higher than I
    Where Your steadfast love is King
    "And Your truth reaches to the skies."
    My life may be a mess
    But You, my LORD, are great
    And Your greatness overcomes
    My overcomplicated state.
    So take me to the Source
    Where my every need's supplied
    And hold me in Your arms
    Whisper, "Everything's all right."

Because You are here it's true
Because You never leave my side
Because You carry me on through
The craziness of life.
So thank You, God, today
Though my stomach's up in knots
I trust You'll get me through
When You are all I've got.

TOO FULL

Father God,
Most glorious Savior
Creator, Redeemer, Sustainer
Will You save me now?
The stress, the worry, the anxiety
The nebulousness of it
The back pain
The stomach knot
The clenched teeth
I don't even know what I'm anxious *about*
Except too many pieces filling up my life:
Am I afraid I won't hold them all together?
Afraid I'll drop one
and my life will shatter
when one
single
piece
hits the floor?
Oh Savior,
with a mind full of full
and no room for peace
because there's no room for You

or anything else besides the words:
"get it done"

I need You
    to replace the nebulous full
    and fill me overflowing with You
    instead.

As a conniving little anxiety attack
    waits but a thought process away
    and Satan snickers at the door
    holding a chain for me -
    Free me, Savior, I beg!
    I don't know how to be free
    except by Your Hand.

I remember:
    You provide
    You protect
    You call me
    to cease striving
    and know
    You are God.

YOUR NAME

"*Those who know Your name will put their trust in You, for You, O LORD, have not forsaken those who trust You*" (Psalm 9:10 NASB).

What is Your name?
   The name which I can trust?
   The name that shows me who I am
   When You call me in Your love?

Your name is power
   Your name is peace
   Your name is Comforter
   Your name is stronghold
   Mighty One
   Who calmed the raging storm.

Your name is great high King
   Your name is Majesty

Your name is Ruler over all
Creator of the sky and sea.
Your name is greatest love
The source of all that's right
Your name is Father, Comforter
Our beacon of the purest Light.

Arise, oh Lord
Declare Your name
May we kneel before Your mighty throne
And praise Your holy, holy name!

I can tell of what You've done
You've worked wonders in my life
I know You'll hold me to the end
Carry me through joy and strife.
Though Satan is my enemy
And man fails to be my friend
You are faithful, You are sure
So I can go where You will send.
You are steadfast, Holy God,
Your love, oh it staggers me!
I've seen You working day by day
And when I forget, Your Name covers me.

For You are good, Your gentleness!
I can never earn Your gaze
Much less Your suffering for me.

As my rhyme and rhythm fail

Just this, I love You, God,
The brokenness of my pen
Will always fail to express
What Your love has done for me
And when I cannot see the change
I'll trust You, God, inside of me.

BUILDING IN THE STORM

"*And after you have suffered a little while, the God of all grace, who has called you to His eternal glory in Christ, will Himself restore, confirm, strengthen, and establish you*" (1 Peter 5:10 NASB).

I'm a fixer, a producer
    A much efficient worker
    And You made me to rejoice in work.
    But when the storms come rolling
    The rain starts pouring
    And I hear that thunder crash
    You are the shelter that I need
    You are the safe place
    You beckon me with outstretched arms
    Into Your house of grace
    But somehow I am blinded -
    Am I deaf to Your calls?
    While the storm rages
    Wets me through and through
    And You call for me to come,
    I fix my efforts instead

On two endeavors of my own:
Stop the storm with my mind
And build a shelter for myself.
The materials I cobble together
Are soaked and second rate
Lightning zaps me as I work
But even that does not deter me
And as I work and try mind control
I call to You across the storm,
"Help me build my safety, I pray!
And stop the storm coming!"
But You know my pathetic shelter
Won't save me from the storm,
And stopping all the rain
Won't help me know You more.
So You let it come, and as it does
You trek through the thunderous plain,
Taking my arm gently so I see,
And then You pull me with You
Patiently with so much grace
And once I'm in Your house
I can listen to Your voice.

It's a time to know You here
    To rest and rejuvenate.
    Sometimes my work is not the answer
    But *You*, my Creator, always are.

A WRESTLING MATCH

"*Therefore there is now no condemnation for those who are in Christ Jesus. For the law of the Spirit of life in Christ Jesus has set you free from the law of sin and of death*" (Romans 8:1-2 ESV).

The scale stands before me
Imposing, condemning
The reason I feel pressure
Pressure to always get it right
Run the house smoothly
Strategize to get and keep it nice
Be patient with my daughters
Teach them well
Raise them right.
Make time for my husband,
Don't make him last in life.
Think of others, be a friend.
Do my job perfectly
Write my story just right.
Give my best to everything.
Be efficient, save the money.
Make everything the best it can be.

Make time for God
Grow in Christ
Don't be negative or discouraged
Just do everything just right.

But darn it -
So often I'm not perfect
- Like every single day -
And as my mantra is try harder
I see the scale in my mind
It's weighted against me I think
'Cause everything I try
I can't learn lessons permanently.
I mess up all the time.
I'm dwelling in this in-between
Of darkness and light
Of death and life
Of sin and right.
Because I know You saved me!
You died to take my place
You brought me out of darkness
And into glorious light.
But I'm in this middle ground
And oh, I hate it so
With that scale always before me
Weighted far against my soul.

BUT

You don't let me oppress myself
You don't leave me in the mire

One day I'm talking to my family
And You lift Satan's blindfold from my eyes:
I'm firmly a dweller
Of the sphere of light and life and right
That's where I live, where I belong
Though I act like I'm in the other sphere,
I'm not.
Satan tries to blind me
But You give me Truth:
You paid for me to dwell here -
I'm a citizen of Light.

And that scale?
The one that I let rule my life?
That scale is weighted against me, I say
To which my mom-in-law replies,
"There is no scale."

Christ satisfied that scale
And removed it.

There is no scale.

The relief that floods my soul
And runs out through my eyes -
I'm free!
My mistakes, shortcomings, repeated sins
Are not weighted against me
For You satisfied the scale
Permanently for me

It has no place in this sphere
Of light and life and right
Where You made me a citizen
A daughter.

Thank You.

TINY JOY

*O*h God, the joy
      Life is joy
Daughters lying by my side
A thoughtful husband, too
Your love is great!
I see it all around
Your magnificent care
The dimple in her elbow
Matches the dimple in her cheek
She hangs on to her milk cup
As if for dear, dear life
She expresses herself around it
Laughs and points and grunts
All with that spout tightly clamped
Between her pearly teeth
Her precious little fingers
Oh so very strong
Grasp my bookmark with steel grip
A moment in time -
A tiny daughter -
Not tiny for much longer.

Thank You for tininess
And moments like these

STARS OF MORNING

*A*s the first stars of morning
       twinkle brightly on
the grey blue sky illumines
the stately grey, leafless trees.
The changing of the light every morning
You created such a beautiful daily dance
that I love for the quiet peace, stillness inside.
Just watch, let it sink in!
The coming of the day!
I don't have to fuss or flurry, scramble or scrape

-

     just sit and smile
     welcome and marvel.

You are good.

The daily turn reminds me
     of Your faithfulness - daily
     You will not change -
     though I do:

my heart, my focus, my concerns
but You are faithful ever.
And as I change
You hold onto me
You draw me back
when I wander, distracted
by shiny or scaly
You draw me back
back to Life.

Thank You for never letting go
    never losing me
    never giving me up
    or losing interest.

Thank You for holding me.

YOUR MERCY

God, Your mercy is unfathomable
   Your glory is unending
    You rescue the broken and deserted
You do what we believe impossible.
Your Creation reflects Your glory
The mountains rise in majesty
The stars flood the sky
Jupiter marches magnificently
With Saturn following
Twirling in its rings like a gown
The sun rises in blazes
And sets in pastels
There's a rhythm to all You made
Even the wildfires bring life
No matter how we pollute
And desecrate this land
It still sings forth Your power
And the beauty of Your hand
We take it all for granted
Till we stop and catch our breath
And feel it taken from us
In a rush of excitement and awe

What glory all around us
Reminds me of Your plan
The silliness of discontent
When my life is in Your Hand.
And *this* is what You've given
Family, friends, and laughs
Beauty to soak in daily
And simple joys of life.
Thank You.

PRINCE

*J*esus, You are the Prince of Peace.
What does that mean for me?
That -
Even in my turmoil
Even in my mess
Even in my loneliness
When I feel the weight of responsibility
crushing me under
You are my Prince
You are my Peace.
And You are Wonderful Counselor!
When my mind is confused
My emotions awry
My path greyed out
My future foggy
You are worthy of awe and wonder,
my Counselor!
And You will lead me on
And protect me
For You are Mighty God
Creator of all
The One who designed the sun

And stopped the earth for Joshua.
You blind and create light
Your will is always done.
Eternal Father, Your promises are true
Always and forever.
Your ways are steadfast
Faithful
Since before time began
And forevermore -
And You love me.

I kneel again in humbled awe
    Prince of Peace,
    Everlasting Father,
    Mighty God,
    Wonderful Counselor.

FLEETING

*T*hank You for cozy days
      Hot chocolate
Teddy bears
And instruments.
My babies are so blessed!
They don't know what it is
To be in need of anything at all
To ache with hunger
Or be sick without doctor or medicine.

Today, Lord God,
    Be with the babies
    Who know all that too well.
    Be with the parents
    Who yearn to give them more.
    Give them all *You*.

And I beg, Father,
    Bring my babies to You,

For worldly goods, full bellies, presents under a
tree,
    and healthcare
    Are worthless
    If they don't have eternity.

Our lives are fleeting
    Our time is short
    Help us love one another,
    And help us follow You.

COME, EMMANUEL

O come, Emmanuel
God with us
You are

O come Emmanuel
I ache for
Your return

O come Emmanuel
Our world so angry
So afraid

O come Emmanuel
Bring peace in us
We pray

O come Emmanuel

God with us!
You are!

O come Emmanuel
Reign in my heart
Today

LIKE MARY

*Y*ou told Mary Your favor was on her
You told Mary You were there
You told her, "do not be afraid"
You told her, "*Jesus* you will bear!"
She did not know who Jesus was
She did not know about His reign
She probably thought in earthly terms
A king to end their earthly shame!
But she listened and she accepted
Though no one else would understand
She chose obedience and submission
And then, oh God, she saw Your Hand!
For even Joseph her betrothed
Was stopped from putting her away
You provided for that trusting mama
As she bowed her will to You that day.
And later as her cousin sang,
And shepherds, kings bowed down
Simeon and Anna prophesied
What marvel Mary must have found!
It says in Luke she treasured them
"All these things" - "in her heart"

She must have pondered through the years
What a humble yet exalted start!
You showed us through them a truth
You do not follow our culture's norms
You are not bound by our traditions
Our class systems, prejudices, or scorns.
No, You will come as You may
A King in a stable, humbly born
What matters is not our earthly status
For even You died in a crown of thorns.
But You didn't tell that to little Marry
You didn't tell her how He'd die
You told her what she should know
You would guard her heart where treasured
memories lie.
You gave her the hope for *all* mankind
You placed Him in her arms
You told her the hope that He would bring
And she placed her life in *Your* arms.

May I be like Mary.

WALK

*Y*ou know this walk is hard
    You walked it, too.
    You know the "weakness of our
frame,"
    The temptation to stop
    To veer off into the shallows
    Of muck "pleasures"
    Instead.

You were tempted, too, Jesus.

You know.
    You know the temptation to stop
    To weep and wallow in self-pity
    To take a break from God and His hard path.
    The temptation to forget
    That in that hard path
    Lies freedom
    Joy
    Fulfillment

Because You are there.
You hold my hand
You are there
And You are here, too.
Calling me back
Seeking the lost lamb
When I selfishly, stupidly stray
Because I belong
To You.

KNOWN

*G*od,
    You know me completely and in-
    timately
You made me personally
Intentionally
And You care
Deeply.
I rejoice over our children
Their successes
Their tries
Their choices to forego sin.

You joy and glory in me
    When I reflect little pinpricks of Your Light
    Show Your character in even the smallest ways
    You rejoice!
    You work on me without fail
    Encourage me as I try
    and fail
    or hurt
    Hold me to comfort me and heal me

And You stretch me beyond
Beyond
Beyond
What I think I can do or be.
You are ever
Making me
Who You made me
To be.
And You won't give up.

"He doesn't compare us to anyone else. He doesn't have a list of what Christians should be and do at certain phases of their Christian walk. He accepts us individually and works with us where we are. Yet He constantly challenges us to go beyond what we are. And He throws a great big party whenever we reach a milestone or make a yo-yo spiritual break-through. Why? Because we belong to Him. We BELONG to Him" (*Having a Mary Spirit,* Joanna Weaver, 198).

COME QUICKLY

Oh God.
     My heart aches tonight.
I picture precious moments
Rocking my baby
Cuddling my toddler
Soothing their night time anti-sleep
While the country rages
This country I once called peaceful
Secure
Stable
At least for me.
I realize my dependence
On my oh so easy life
I take for granted safety
Bounty
Love.
Oh God
These are blessings that some only have in heaven!
But I get to taste
-a flawed taste-
Of them here.

And I take that for granted.
God
Tonight my heart aches.
For my illusions
Shattered
For my brothers and sisters
Oppressed
For my brothers and sisters
Oppressing
For those who grieve
For those who hate,
Whose hearts shrivel
Who are captive to Your Enemy and mine
And they don't know.
So they hate
And they rage
And they justify all
And are led further from Life and Light.
Oh God,
Bring Your light!
Shine on us all
Show us how to help the hurting
How to love the oppressor
How to cling to You
Our Rock
And our Redeemer
Through it all.
Come quickly, Lord Jesus.

COMPASSION

ear God,

Will you make me compassionate?
    For the person who calls
    Looking for food, complaining to me that life isn't fair.
    I don't know her
    But You do.
    Give me compassion
    So I can give her You.

Will You make me compassionate?
    Like my sweet husband
    Who knows how to reach our daughter
    When she's giving a show of anger, stubbornness, and self-will
    Give me compassion
    So I can give her You.

. . .

Will you make me compassionate?
 When Satan temps me to judge:
 "If they just did THIS
 Everything would be better!"
 "Wow. They're totally crazy."
 Instead,
 Will You give me compassion
 So I can be like You?

FAITHFUL

Faithful
        God help me be faithful
When my emotions fail
When I sink
When I feel the words
FAIL FAILURE FAILED
Stamped on my soul
You are here
And I am not the point
When my self becomes the center
Failure is the outcome
I'm not meant to be the center
That space is Your domain.
You belong there
You reign from there
Life is RIGHT
When I remember You are there.
So bring me to my right place
In Your arms
As Your child
Who stumbles and falls
And is rejuvenated and growing

In You.
Thank You for being my Father
Who loves me without frowns
Guides me with patience
Upholds me with Your hand.
Thank You

CLEANING HOUSE

When the stillness of night
Gently gives way to the dawn
And the stars fade from my view
I remember how easy it is
To slowly lose sight of You.
My mind is such a full house
It seems I just push things aside
To make room for You in the morning
Then the clutter moves back to reside.
But I ponder now and I think perhaps
What I really ought to do
Is glory in a thorough spring cleaning
So I can clear the house for You.
Will You help me do this?
To junk the junk and not look back?
To organize and strategize
But mostly, dear Father
To open the whole house to You?
So that as the clutter trickles back in
You can help me clear it out
As Master of my house and Lord of my heart
Take my will and make it Yours

So I can do what You're about!

Thank You for the stars this predawn
    That display Your glory with heralding voice
    Unrivaled magnitude and magnificence
    You, oh God, are beyond my words.
    What joy brims up in me because of that!
    My utter lack, my glory.
    For then I glory in You only
    The Creator of the universe, of my mind, my
soul.

May I not be distracted by what to do
    Unless it's Your telling
    I want to just sit here
    And BE
    In You

REASON

*Y*ou have me here
    For a reason
    For a purpose
Probably multiple reasons, purposes.
You have me in this city
This neighborhood
These jobs
Around these people
With these friends
In this church
With children this old
In this time of life
For Your purposes
And my good
And I pray -
For the good of those around me.

I'm here
    Not because I love it
    Or to make it my forever home
    Or to feel satisfied in life

Or make a perfect show home
Or measure up to friends or magazine pictures
Or be the best, the admired.
No, Your purposes are so far beyond such nonsense.
We'd rather play in mudpies
Than live in Your house,
C.S. Lewis said.
We trade Your glory
Your peace
Your joy
For trinkets
Idols that don't satisfy
Obsession with looks
Money
Cultural standards.
But You are full of the riches of grace!
All glory!
All power!
All contentment - TRUE contentment
All peace
All love.

And I trade You for mud.

You have me *here*.

I want to see You.
I want to be blinded by Your glory
So that none else satisfies.
No momentary lies
Or temptations

Will move me then.

Oh God, when You bring me truly HOME…

But for now
    You have me here.
    So draw me ever closer
    Loving Papa
    Almighty God
    Faithful Father
    Glorious Savior -
    Draw me near to You.

VALLEY OF VISION
PONDERING

When I am sick
   I find You in these old old words
Penned by Puritans of faith
Broken people
With a difficult modern reputation
But these words of faith
And humility
Live on
To encourage
To give steadfastness
To lift our eyes
To You.
You are great, oh God!
Through all generations
All peoples broken in different ways
You are the same yesterday, today, and tomorrow
And Your faithfulness reaches to the skies.
You are glorious beyond compare
Yet stoop to bestow grace upon us
You are almighty
Yet lend strength to our weak bodies and souls

You are indescribably holy
Yet dwelt among sinners
And died by their hands
So we could be holy too.
All praise to You

Wonderful
    Counselor
    Mighty God
    Everlasting Father
    Prince of peace.

FALL

*G*od
How magnificent is Your creation!
Just a sliver of what You've made
And I feel my breath catching
My heart beats slower and stress melts
As I behold Your artistry.
Sometimes
I think that's what autumn is for
Living in awe
Of the colors
The tapestry
The circle of nature
As summer flies away
with the golden, crimson, flaming leaves.
How beautiful it is!
How incredible You are
All the workings that are too small
Too intricate
For me to see.
That reminds me of all that is going on
In my life
In others' lives

That I can't see
That I don't comprehend yet.
But You are orchestrating it all
It's all in Your hands.

Thank You for fall.

COVENANT CHILD

*Y*ou created her to be free
    She was born into bonds of sin
    But also born a covenant child
Who we know is in Your hands
You created her
To come to You
The truest of Loves
And lay down her loves
Desires
Hatreds
Temptations
Sins
And be free
Truly Free
In You!

So when she prayed that prayer
    When she called on Your name
    Though she doesn't fully understand
    (Neither do I!)
    She is fully Yours.

Oh God!
Fully Yours!
She is not bound
Even when Satan tells her she's chained
She's free in You!
Your spirit lives inside the baby
Who You let me borrow
For a short time.
Oh God,
Good and kind Maker
Lord of the universe
Creator of all
She belongs to You
And that is
Joy.
Free, abandoned joy -
Guard her, Father
And help me guide her
Always
To You.

THE PIANO

*T*he joy
        that bubbles inside
when I see
little hands
beside the ones
that I studied
thirteen years ago,
my heart drawn
to the man they belong to
as he played
Skillet
Plumb
Andrew Lloyd Webber
Simple Plan.
His voice
smooth and clear
sang the notes
and I joined him.
He and his music pursued me
won me
and with inexpressible joy
I watch

as our second daughter follows his lead.
Her tiny hands gently pound the keys,
her atonal melody joins his song,
as she watches,
learns from Daddy,
and makes her own music.
Her chubby little legs dangle from the bench,
her brows furrow as she plays,
and when she lifts her wordless voice,
my heart is lifted too.

Perhaps God,
    You'll remind me,
    Someday when she is tall
    that though she may sing a similar song to
mine,
    Your melody for her is unique -
    and I don't know it yet.
    My job is not to make her song mine
    to make her composition match the song
I've sung
    but instead to give her to You,
    point her to the Great Composer,
    Creator of the vast score of the universe,
    who writes every note,
    conducts every instrument,
    and uses our squeals and missed notes
    in His grand design.
    You know the melody she'll follow,
    and I'll trust You'll hold the hands
    with which she plays
    and with which she writes.

. . .

You know
    You direct
    and You are good.

Remind me when I'm lost
    in my own sheet music
    trying to glance at hers
    scared of the notes she plays.
    Remind me
    that You hold the score
    and her melody is there.

For now,
    thank You for tiny hands
    a lisping tongue,
    wordless shouts and giggles.

Thank You for our baby.

THE ARTIST

A photo cannot capture
     The ultimate
Glorious color
The pinpricks of design
The delicate veins that stripe
The breathtaking beauty
The Artist You are!
Thank You for this moment
A tiny slice in time
A pause in my day
To see
To marvel
To glorify
The eternal Artist
Who paints for all
No need for notice or applause
Just Joy
That's what I see today in this changing tree -
Joy

MY WELL

Father,
       When I feel distant and confused
Not close to You as I desire
When I'm wandering and foggy
Is this a thorn?
A chance to obey and seek?
Or is it just a call
To spend more time with You
For that's when the closeness comes -
When I rest in You.
You are the Well
You are the Source
You are my Peace
You are my King.
And when my focus is is elsewhere
Of course I feel lost
Discontent
Because I'm supposed to be
With You.
I was made
For communion with You
Walking with You daily

As Adam and Eve did in the garden
I'm not perfect as they were
But You made a way for me to walk with You too.
Jesus
Thank You
For making a way
Thank You for walking with me
Carrying me
Calling me back
To where I belong:
With You.

IT'S FEAR

*A*re we stewarding wisely?
      Spending well?
Saving better?
Am I the best mom I can be?
Am I patient?
Kind?
Educational?
Will I get it all done?
Is my house the best it can be?
Am *I* the best I can be?
Am I memorable?
Valuable?
Am I worthwhile?

These questions:
    One motive behind them all:
    Fear.

I long to be valuable
    To be valued

But I fear
I'm not.
I'm not enough.

But God

You are enough
    Enough for both of us
    And You love me
    You value me
    I am enough
    For You
    Always.

Even when I know I'm failing
    Even when I disappoint others
    Even when I sin again and again
    You love me
    You value me
    You uphold me.
    Thank You for freeing me
    For giving me the sword
    To cut off fear's head
    Every time it rears
    And the more I swing my sword
    - feebly at first, it's true -
    The more You strengthen my muscle
    The quicker the sword swings
    And stronger
    Next time.
    And the smaller that fear gets
    The more timidly it rears

For You are fear-Crusher
And You have given me Your sword.

"In all circumstances take up the shield of faith...the helmet of salvation, and the sword of the Spirit, which is the Word of God, praying at all times..." (Ephesians 6:16-18).

GUIDE

*G*od,
    Will You help us as we try to guide our
    girls in their talents?
Show us their passions, the sparks in their souls
And help us leave our pride on the floor
Stomp on it, destroy it
So it has naught to do with our guiding.
Give us eyes to see them the way You do
Instead.

Thank You!
    For their precious gifts already showing!
    God, they're so wonderful.
    Give me patience with them, please?
    Please halt the impatience
    the frustrated tones of voice
    the mad words
    before they venture out
    to hurt, to shut down.

. . .

Thank You for guiding *us*
and providing as we in turn guide them.
Great Waymaker, lead us on today.

SPIRITUAL BATTLE

"*For we do not wrestle against flesh and blood, but against the rulers, against the authorities, against the cosmic powers over this present darkness, against the spiritual forces of evil in the heavenly places*" (Ephesians 6:12 ESV).

My battle is not with flesh or blood
    With pee on the carpet and soaked socks
    With obstinate words thrown at me:
    "But I don't *want* to be kind!"
    (I don't either right now, sweet daughter)
    With piles of crusty dishes or pee-wet laundry
    With sugar yearnings or bedtime crazies
    With home fixes and storage issues
    With money questions and stewardship…

No.

My battle is against

"the rulers,
against the powers,
against the world forces
of this darkness,
against the spiritual forces of wickedness
in the heavenly places."

This pee-soaked floor is a battle for my soul.

Will I sigh and silent-rage?

Will I wallow in self-pity, complain to my husband?

Take a picture for Instagram to get some sympathy?

Or

Will I cling - fiercely - to You?

Will I find my kindness
the love I need
the patience I strive for
in You?

Will I submit to *Your* authority
instead of to Satan's tempting?

Will I show love and compassion
when my first instinct is to say,

"I *told* you that would happen!"

and

"It's your own fault. Stop crying."

and

"If you didn't ___, *that* wouldn't have happened."

Oh God.

You call me higher
and oh, to such better.

You call me to Your joy
You call me to call them
invite them
show them
You.
How can I do that with prideful words?
When I focus on my own rightness and her
mistakes?
You call me higher.
Thank You
for not having my own attitude with *me*.
Help me switch it out
for Your response of genuine love
instead.
Please, Father,
Give me Your love
for my daughters.

A MOMENT OF REALIZATION

*G*od,
    You know us completely and in-
    timately.
You made us personally
intentionally,
and You care
deeply.

When we rejoice over our children
    their successes
    their tries
    their choices to forego sin,
    it reminds me:
    You joy and glory in us
    when we reflect little pinpricks of Your light,
    show Your character in even the smallest ways -
    You rejoice!
    You work on us without fail,
    encourage us as we try or fail or hurt,
    hold us to comfort us and heal us.
    And You stretch us beyond

beyond
beyond
what we think we can do or be.
You are ever
making us
who You made us
to be.
And
You won't
give up.

REROUTE ME

*R*eroute me, God,
All those intricate firings in my brain.
Reroute me, Creator
When I find myself
On that path again.
That path I trod so readily
- So silly of me really -
The self-pity path is filled with briars,
Thorns, sharp stones, and quick sand.
And at the end of it?
A deadly cliff.
Yet I veer there quite often:
"I do *everything* around here!"
"I'm so tired - everyone else gets all the sleep!"
"They have no idea how much I really do."
- Thorns, pricking myself until I bleed.
Briars, tangling myself in destructive thoughts.
Quicksand.
And I'm wallowing as I drown.
I veer because I follow the whispers,
Satan's whispers and lies.

But Your Spirit calls me gently back:
"It's better over here.
Come do it all for Me instead."

For when I remember what You teach
    What Paul said in Colossians 3:23-24 (NASB):
    "Whatever you do, do your work heartily,
    as for the Lord rather than for men,
    knowing that from the Lord you will receive
    the reward of the inheritance.
    It is the Lord Christ whom you serve."
    Then I can breathe -
    When I do it all for You
    You see, You care, You wrap Your arms
around me
    And help me laugh it through.
    Thank You, God, for that freedom and peace.

VICTORY

"*For God has not given us a spirit of fear, but of power and of love and of a sound mind*" (1 Timothy 1:7 NASB).

You are Fear-Crusher
You are Sin-Slayer
You are Triumphant God!
And You've given me Your sword.
I want to walk Your path,
Live Your Word
But I can't seem to get it right
Not without You, Lord.
I need a new weapon
My fists won't seem to do
All this puny strength of mine
It can't, can't -
Jesus, I need You!
I'm afraid of my failure
Afraid every day
I'm afraid of this world
All the hate that comes my way
I'm afraid of my wayward tongue
Of the words I tend to say

So I'm running to You now, God
I throw myself on You and pray:
You are Fear-Crusher
You are Sin-Slayer
You are Triumphant God!
And You've given me Your sword.
Oh God, how often I forget
The power in Your hands
Day by day You give Your weapon
And by my side You stand
So all I need to do
Is see You by my side
Ask You for Your strength…
patience…wisdom
And swing with all my might!
For You are Fear-Crusher
You are Sin-Slayer
You are Triumphant God!
And You've given me Your sword.
The more I choose to swing
O so feeble sometimes it's true
But the more I stand my ground and swing
Drawing vital strength from you
I feel those muscles harden
Your Words comes to mind more often
And before I know it, Lord,
You've made me more like You!
And You are Fear-Crusher
You are Sin-Slayer
You are Triumphant God!
And You've given me Your sword.

PURPOSE

"*Therefore, if you have been raised up with Christ, keep seeking the things above, where Christ is, seated at the right hand of God. Set your mind on things above, not on the things that are on earth*" (Colossians 3:1-2 NASB).

"*You will seek Me and find me when you search for Me with all your heart*" (Jeremiah 29:13 NASB).

Your purposes are beautiful
    Your purposes are kind
    Sometimes I fail to see them
    Or understand them with my mind
    But they're still so beautiful
    You're still merciful and true
    Your faithfulness astounds me
    When I stop and rest in You.
    So God, keep molding me and plotting
    My every day's design
    Encourage me to trust You
    And cling to You each time:
    Each time I'm tempted elsewhere

Each time I'm lost and scared
Each time I feel resentment
Each time I'm heart-impaired.
I smile as I remember
Those time - You're *here* with me
No matter where my mind is
You're calling patiently.
I joy in that blessed call
For God, You are so kind!
I'll rest in You this moment
And hope in You I'll find.

OUTSIDE AND INSIDE

I look out and I see people:
    Broken
  Trying
  Wrong
  Hurting
  Angry
  Fearful
  Scraping
  Blaming
  Sin-stained.

I look inside me and see I'm:
    Broken
    Trying
    Wrong
    Hurting
    Angry
    Fearful
    Scraping
    Blaming
    Sin-stained.

Hopeless, the same.

I look again with God's hope at them and at me:
    God's image
    Little reflections
    Glimmer of You
    Your character.
    Broken bits of glass,
    Reflections of You are everywhere
    It's not hopeless
    I look at me and see:
    Forgiven
    by You
    Loved
    by You
    Stainless
    Hope-filled
    In-dwelt by You.

And outside?
    Many, like me
    Others, blind to what You offer to them.
    Stumbling in that blindness
    Angry,
    Fearful
    Shamed
    Hurt
    Weeping
    Because of the sin-stain
    The blindness.

Why am I here?

To reach them!
To encourage those like me who have
Your hope
To offer Your Light and healing to the blind
To love all broken people with everything
I have
And more
Because I also draw from You
The everlasting Love.

You are faithful, You are good
Forgive me for making a self-serving cave
in which to dwell.
Give me Your love
Your sight
Your wisdom
Your desire for the lost.
Give me You
And lead me in Your ways.

THE LOST

God,
Today I saw a friend's post
Missing her dad
Who died awhile back.
It reminded me of all the people who die
Day after day.
Sometimes they are ones we love achingly
And we don't know if they were Yours.
God,
I'm so sheltered by robust LIFE in this country
So barely touched by death
And I forget
- oh so easily I forget! -
that death comes to ALL.
The stranger on the street
My neighbors next door
My best friends
My parents
My children
All.

. . .

I forget.

And the problem with this blind forgetfulness
    The problem with this life-ful culture
    The problem with our health idolatry
    Is that we ignore the death coming for everyone
    And that means we forget their eternal souls.
    Oh God,
    I forget my neighbor has a soul!
    I forget that someday - maybe even today! -
    She will be called to account for her life
    And if she has not trusted Jesus and surrendered to Him
    She will be eternally lost.

God,
    I can wrestle with this
    Rebel against the idea
    Ask You why and how come
    But that won't change the truth
    And it won't change my lukewarm witness to my neighbor
    Who daily draws closer to death.

Will You change me, God?
    Will You give me a heart for the lost?

YOUR CALL

*Y*ou call me to patience
      You call me to trust
        To cast aside fear
To leave behind worry
To rest in Your plan
And see Your glory.
When I focus on doing those things
I fail
Another checklist scribbled out
But that's forgetting who *You* are!
You don't call me to just *do*
You call me to *abide.*
To settle in with You
Remember and learn
Who You are.

You are God.

You are Creator

Who saw Your Creation go to pieces in their freedom
And loved them enough
To clothe them in soft skins
To banish them from fulfilling perfection
So they'd find their fulfillment
Their perfection
Only in You.
They'd cast it
and You
aside.
But You didn't do the same to them.
Instead, You made a Way
For them
For us
For me
To be in You
With You
Always.
And nothing I do
Will screw that up.
Including unchecked checklists
Impatience
Anger
Worry
Inefficiency
Lack of stewardship
Depression
Failed productivity.

We can't mess up Your perfect sacrifice
Or Your perfect plan.
You died for me.
You've made the Way.

And as I find myself in You
Remembering who You are
I find that I am able
By clinging to Your Hand
To do today.

A TEEN TIME

I will speak of You!
   It's the best my faulty tongue can do:
To tell of You.

I remember a time when I grew older
   Barely a teen perhaps
   There was something I wanted
   I don't remember what it was
   But I do remember You graciously gave it
   When Mom suggested I just ask You.
   Immediately You showed Yourself
   A loving Father who pours blessings on His children
   Who are just beginning
   To know You personally.
   What a kind Father You are!

Around that same time
   You began the tug
   That pulled us to Africa

Proving once again
That Your design for our lives
Is so much better than we could dream or plan.
None of us even wanted to visit Africa
But You will get us on track
Despite ourselves
And then *we* reap the blessings.

STEADFAST

Oh make my heart steadfast, my God,
        May my lips speak Your praises all
the day
    May all see Your glory through my witness
    May my daughters follow after You
    As they see Your work in our lives.
    Oh my God, You are so mighty!
    We see Your Hand every single day
    As we read these missionary stories
    We sit in awe, spines tingling,
    Hearing Your miracles, Your faithfulness,
    Your love for Your people!
    God, we want to fill our minds with You
    So we do not stray, distracted by the world.
    So make our hearts steadfast, I pray.

UNHIDDEN

*O*h God, Father, and Creator
　　I look to You now
As I recognize fears clenching my stomach
Invading my mind in the night.
I did not realize it was fear
That instructed my mind to race
To think of ways to control
To fix
To make all right
In panic mode
Not letting me rest in You
Hiding the truth of Your Word
Hiding the fact that I was lost in fear.
I cried out to You for mercy
Longing for sleep
And You answered me.
Then, blessing larger still,
You revealed to me what was hiding under
a rock
Snakelike and devious:
The fear, disguised.
You revealed the serpent

And You don't leave me to fight it alone
With bare, shaking hands
Or brittle sticks of my own controlling plans
That break and feed the fear
When they hit its glistening fangs.
No,
You stay with me,
My Knight in shining armor,
You are at my side
You flip the rock
Revealing the Enemy
You hold my hand
You give me Your sword
And as I make timid, striking blows,
The Fear begins to slither away
and flee.
But I look to You
For I know it will return
A different disguise perhaps
Next time
But I look to You
Fear Crusher
Snake Slayer
Please slay the serpent
Crush the fear
In me.

JOHN 15:5

"*Apart from Me, you can do nothing*" (John 15:5 NASB).

I am not apart from You -
    Praise God!
    Praise the Son!
    Praise You, Holy Spirit!
    Because I am not apart from You.
    You are in me,
    whether I remember Your Presence or not
    You are with me.
    You promised never to leave
    And You are here.
    Here, as I write against the steering wheel
    Overlooking the brown field and marsh
    Rain pouring down on trees beginning
    to push forth buds
    Here in my weariness
    My done-ness
    My mind cloudiness
    Here where I am

How I am
Right now.
And You will not leave.
Though I forget Your power, Your Presence
Though I rely on my own insufficiency
Though I lose my temper
and speak sharply to the precious gifts called
children
whom You gave us to protect, serve, and love
Though I am selfish
Though I am weak,
You are in me.
You are here.
Never to leave
Never to forsake
Even when my priorities are wrong
You are here
in me
Thank You.

FEAR CRUSHER

*Y*ou are Fear-Crusher
    You are Light-Maker
    You make the darkness flee
You are Sky Holder
Bird Tender
Gentle Shepherd of Your sheep.
You won't let the darkness win
When it's creeping over me
And You hold the sickness back
When I'm sick with misery.
Oh God, You're Fear-Crusher!
Love Dealer
You are my only Hope
And I cling to You right now
With joy rising in my soul.
I don't have to sink on down
Or drown in the mess
'Cause my Knight lives here in me:
I can trust Your faithfulness.
'Cause You are Fear-Crusher!
Light Maker!
You've made the darkness flee

I will cling to You in hope
Through this adversity.
Fear Crusher
Love Dealer
Faithful Knight and King
God, You are my hope and King.

MY LACK

The exhaustion is what I fear
        It takes away my control
I fear losing control
of my anger
of my mind
Because things become cloudy when I'm tired
I lose my clarity
And my emotions are much stronger
And I become weak.
So I am afraid
Afraid - to be tired.

But now I remember
        The story I heard
        The man, full of Your Spirit
        diagnosed with a brain tumor.
        His response?
        "Thank You, God!
        Now I can't think my way out.
        I must rely completely
        totally

on You."

That is the faith You call me to
    That is the faith You give
    So I ask You for that faith today
    That through exhaustion I may live
    And seek Your will through the haze.

Thank You for my lack.

REMEMBER

*R*emember -
Oh help me remember, God!
Your faithfulness and love
How You provide and protect
The way You sustain me
Little me, exhausted and worn
You put Your Spirit in me
You see fit to dwell in *me*
Little forgetful me
And You treat me as precious
Valuable
Worthwhile
Simply because You choose to
Because I'm Yours.

Help me shine Your Light
Your Love
Today.

Help me remember.

ETERNAL

*G*od,
My emotions feel untamed,
Wild as an unbroken horse
Sometimes gentle, playful, happy,
Other times, unruly, unmanageable,
Rearing with fear and anger and rebellion.
My body does things I don't understand:
Why am I so hot at night?
Why can't I sleep?
Why the mood swings?
But You are faithful! You are good.
You lead me in the way everlasting.
This body, these hormones, won't last.
This shell will whither, break, fade
I do not put my hope in its temporary health
and strength.
No indeed, for I have a God
Who is eternal
Who makes promises everlasting
Who pours lavish, eternal, unchanging love
over me
Daily

Who upholds my feeble frame
Provides for, feeds, clothes it.
All the while feeding me the living water
Because I am eternal
And I have the hope of heaven
Through Your Son's sacrifice.
This day,
May I remember eternity
And place my trust in You.

THOUSANDS

A thousand thoughts and to-do's
    Swirl in my brain
Perhaps to write them down would help -
But no, a thousand takes up too much white space.
    I want to live a life for You
    Purposeful and free
    I want to be a shining light.

I want to live shining, fully me
    I want to make an impact
    Do great good in this world
    And right now I'm spinning crazy
    Too scattered to do much good
    So I grasp this moment
    Hold now with both my hands
    Close my eyes, abide in You,
    Worship with all I've got.
    God, You are good - so good
    And faithful, loving, too.
    Your arms 'round me are strong enough

To hold me together even in a swirling, scattered mess
    You hold the planets in their orbits
    Watch the deer give birth alone
    The clouds and wind know Your taming Hand
    The squirrels plan as You designed
    They store their food for coming months
    And gorillas can talk with their hands
    You designed them, too.
    Great flaming stars dance and whirl
    Yet never one step out of place
    So too You hold my heart
    My life is kept within Your grace.
    So, God, as I sit here silent with my pen
    Will You take my perfectly-made brain,
    Contain the thoughts that run within
    And shape them, organize them,
    To seek Your face.

HUNGER

Father Creator God,
    Will You grant me manna?
But more so
Will You grant me the daily hunger
For the manna You daily provide?
And more so
Will You give me the grace
to draw me to You every morning
Hungry for the manna
To receive it from Your Hand
Gratefully
Moment by moment -
Daily?
Will You give me the humility and courage
Necessary for that consistent act,
Constant choice?
I want to focus on You!
I want Your perspective
I long for Your eyes to see everything
And everyone
Around me.

Oh God,
I long for *You*.
Bless me with that hunger every day, I pray.

CONFLICT

God,
As I have conflict in my heart
once again
A frustration, a longing to fix
To make him listen, understand
Please change my heart and perspective
Write his story and mine
And help me keep my pen off his page
Trusting Your authorship.

TO DO

*G*od, there's always more to do
   To-do lists to perfect life
   Or at least to do life the best way.
I sit through church
Or wake in the night
The only times my mind is still
Trying to catch up
And the lists trample me
As I try to sleep
Long to worship.
I feel the guilt of not worshiping
Or resting
Or playing fully in the moment
because there's always more to do.

The list parades through my mind.
   Banners waving high:
   "Have you thought about this?
   To be a stellar mom, you gotta keep up!
   No one will do it for you!
   Their biblical training rests on you!

Are you keeping up?
keeping up?
keeping up?"

Father, is this obsession
    This fear
    This frenetic mind
    Overloaded brain
    Depressed spirit
    A symptom of distrust?
    How do I live a life of faith?
    My mind adds:
    "And get it all done right?"
    It's my responsibility to think of
    and do
    all these things,
    right?
    Or do I need to remember that
    You guide me
    You love my family
    You raise my children
    And I am not God.
    I am not You.
    You hold us in Your Hand.
    This life,
    these tired moments,
    these choices
    are a gift.
    This child in front of me,
    with messy curls heaving sighs,
    is a gift.
    And You are all I need.
    You alone are my Judge.

                . . .

My family is Yours.
I am Yours.
I open my hands now
Hold them open to You.
Do with me as You will.
Thank You for the faith to open the hands.

YOUR SWORD

"$\mathcal{I}$*have hidden your word in my heart that I might not sin against you"* (Psalm 119:11 NIV).

"In addition to all this, take up the shield of faith, with which you can extinguish all the flaming arrows of the evil one. Take the helmet of salvation and the sword of the Spirit, which is the word of God" (Ephesians 6:16-17 NIV).

"Jesus said to him, "Away from me, Satan! For it is written: 'Worship the Lord your God, and serve him only'" (Matthew 4:10 NIV).

God,
    I've been so discouraged
    By the war I've waged within
    Temptations snare me so easily
    I fall so quickly into sin.

But God, You are so faithful
You're growing me each day
And Your latest revelation
I thank You for today!
I have Your Word right beside me
I can hide it in my heart.
And when I realize I'm sliding
Reciting gives a quick restart
Because You've given me Your armor
And part of that's Your sword
It's called "Sword of the Spirit"
The sword that is *Your Word.*
It's been broken in already
It's seen the fight of fights
Jesus used it on that mountain
When Satan tried to shift His sights.
But You, the Maker of Creation,
God-man, three-in-one
You used the Holy Scripture
To combat the evil one!
So help me as I charge it up
This awe-some sword of Yours
By memorizing Scripture
True words from Truest Source.

Thank You, God, for Your sword.
    You are so kind to me.
    Your mercy and Your wisdom
    Reach beyond infinity.
    Thank You.

FOR MY DAUGHTER

On a soft, made-to-be-lazy day
          With just a gentle leftover from yester-
day's gale of wind
    I remember yesterday's storm of behavior
    And ask a portion of wisdom for today.
    Will You allot me patience, wise words, or si-
lence for each moment?
    Will You sprinkle patience, consideration, and
gentle love on those curly blonde heads upstairs?
    Will You help them taste and see the joy of
living love instead of selfishness?
    Will You align our priorities with Yours?
    My sweet daughter wants things *just so*, and
people are not that.
    Will You press her close to Your heart
    So she hears its rhythm and echoes its love
    When she feels the breaking of her perfect
setup?
    Her expectations?
    Her idealized world?
    Let her cling to You instead

Trust You enough to love when her work crashes down

And we act against her wishes.

Show her Your perfection so she can be satisfied with You instead,

While still working to make this world beautiful and better,

With the freedom of hope in You.

FOR MYSELF

*G*od,
     Will You give me the patience to stop
     The unselfishness to stop
To take the time, hold it still, and enter their
head and heart space
To speak Your love
instead of my moralisms
To heal instead of doing damage control.
Give me patience to help reconcile.
Give me Your heart.
Thank You for Your Spirit
Your insight
Your help
Your *Presence* always.

MY ALWAYS

God, You are God, and I am not.
You are eternal, unchanging, perfect in
all Your ways
Even - especially? - when I doubt You.
Forgive my doubts,
thank You for forgiving my doubts.
I am blown by the winds:
of culture
of emotions
of discouragement
of mainstream thought
of hormones
of dashed hopes
of hoping in the wrong thing.
But You, oh God, oh Elohim,
You are my strong refuge
unshaken
always kind
always wise
always forgiving
always here
always guiding

and always, always more.

Thank You for the always, God!

Thank You for the moments when You catch me blowing about in the wind

When You hold me close so I can hear Your heartbeat

catch a glimpse of Your perspective

When You anchor me in You.

That You for being my Always.

ACKNOWLEDGMENTS

To my Creator and Sustainer who loved me first and is my Refuge and Strength, to my dear husband who loves me in my worst of times as well as in my best and encourages me always, to my sister who is a call away when I want to share life in all its excitement and sadness, to my father-in-law for teaching me to remind myself of God's truth, to my mom-in-law who is a constant source of kind and clear-thinking advice, to my parents who read every book I send them and laugh and cry with me always, to all the mamas out there walking this journey, too:

    thank you.

ABOUT THE AUTHOR

Britney Dehnert is a mama of a toddler and a preschooler; a wife of a creative musician artist; a writer of poetry, fantasy, children's books, and mysteries; and a thankful daughter of God. She loves variety in all of life, quiet mornings with her daughters exploring their condo wilderness, staff meetings at Panera with her creative husband who does this writing business with her, classes where she teaches high schoolers how to cook and enjoy 19th century literature, and homemade coconut ice cream. Find out more on her website, www.brit neydehnertbooks.com.

MORE OF BRITNEY'S POETRY

You can check out the other books in the *Hold Me, God* series here:

A NICU Mama's Journey in Prayer

A Tired Mama's Journey in Prayer

Want to help more people discover my books? Leaving an honest review on Amazon helps both authors *and* readers! More reviews means the book gets bumped up in searches, and well-described reviews (don't have to be long) tell readers what to expect. I'd really appreciate you taking just a minute to write a quick review telling what you enjoyed and didn't enjoy about this book.

Made in the USA
Middletown, DE
26 November 2022

15796001R20077